The National Intelligence Strategy

of the

United States of America

Transformation through Integration and Innovation

October 2005

Foreword

The new concept of "national intelligence" codified by the Intelligence Reform and Terrorism Prevention Act passed by Congress in 2004 has its origins in the tragedy of September 11, 2001 and President Bush's *National Security Strategy of the United States of America*. The President signed the new law with the expectation that "our vast intelligence enterprise will become more unified, coordinated, and effective." Our charge is clear:

- Integrate the domestic and foreign dimensions of US intelligence so that there are no gaps in our understanding of threats to our national security;

- Bring more depth and accuracy to intelligence analysis; and

- Ensure that US intelligence resources generate future capabilities as well as present results.

Implicit in each of these tasks is the assumption that this new approach to "national intelligence" represents a far-reaching reform of previous intelligence practices and arrangements. National intelligence must be collaborative, penetrating, objective, and far-sighted. It must recognize that its various institutional cultures developed as they did for good reasons while accepting the fact that all cultures either evolve or expire, and the time has come for our domestic and foreign intelligence cultures to grow stronger by growing together.

US national intelligence must be tailored to the threats of the 21st century, which seldom conform to the traditional profiles of hostile states and alliances. Adversarial states have learned to mask their intentions and capabilities, while terrorists and other non-state actors use commonplace technologies to boost their striking power and enhance their elusiveness.

The first order of business for US national intelligence, therefore, is to inform and warn the President, the Cabinet, the Congress, the Joint Chiefs of Staff and commanders in the field, domestic law enforcement and homeland security authorities in the heartland, and our international allies. In this sense, as President Bush has said, intelligence is America's first line of defense, in service to our people, our interests, our values, and our Constitution. But even though the future holds dangerous challenges both within our borders and beyond, it also presents us with opportunities to support the spread of freedom, human rights, economic growth and financial stability, and the rule of law. We must identify these opportunities for democratic transformation because

This new approach to "national intelligence" represents a far-reaching reform of previous intelligence practices and arrangements.

autocratic and failed states are breeding grounds of international instability, violence, and misery. For US national security, democracy is the stoutest pillar of support. Intelligence can and should be used to aid diplomacy, influence potential adversaries prior to crises, help make war an instrument of last resort, and ensure victory in the event that conflict is unavoidable.

At its core, this National Intelligence Strategy capitalizes on the extraordinary talents and patriotism of America's diverse intelligence professionals, those serving today and those joining us tomorrow. This strategy also relies on our nation's tradition of teamwork and technological innovation to integrate the work of our distinct components into collaborative success. It sets forth two kinds of strategic objectives—mission and enterprise—and calls for plans that recognize each Intelligence Community member's core strengths and competencies, and are written in consultation with the relevant departments and agencies. Finally, it states the importance of instituting methods of self-evaluation to ensure that the Intelligence Community meets decision-makers' needs and upholds the rule of law. The emphasis placed here on national intelligence reflects a change in the threats we face as a nation, not a change in our commitment to civil liberties and freedom.

A strategy is a statement of fundamental values, highest priorities, and orientation toward the future, but it is an action document as well. For US national intelligence, the time for change is now. There are no easy answers to the risks contemplated here, or the risks that might emerge. This strategy therefore accepts risk as intelligence's natural and permanent field of action and is based on the proposition that to preserve our security in a dangerous century, vigilance is not enough. US national intelligence must do more.

[signature]

John D. Negroponte
Director of National Intelligence

2

The National Intelligence Strategy of the United States of America

Our Vision—What we will become:

A unified enterprise of innovative intelligence professionals whose common purpose in defending American lives and interests, and advancing American values, draws strength from our democratic institutions, diversity, and intellectual and technological prowess.

Our Mission—What we must do:

- Collect, analyze, and disseminate accurate, timely, and objective intelligence, independent of political considerations, to the President and all who make and implement US national security policy, fight our wars, protect our nation, and enforce our laws.

- Conduct the US government's national intelligence program and special activities as directed by the President.

- Transform our capabilities in order to stay ahead of evolving threats to the United States, exploiting risk while recognizing the impossibility of eliminating it.

- Deploy effective counterintelligence measures that enhance and protect our activities to ensure the integrity of the intelligence system, our technology, our armed forces, and our government's decision processes.

- Perform our duties under law in a manner that respects the civil liberties and privacy of all Americans.

Our strategy is to integrate, through intelligence policy, doctrine, and technology, the different enterprises of the Intelligence Community.

Our Strategy—How we will succeed:

The stakes for America in the 21st century demand that we be more agile and resourceful than our adversaries. Our strategy is to integrate, through intelligence policy, doctrine, and technology, the different enterprises of the Intelligence Community. It encompasses current intelligence activities as well as future capabilities to ensure that we are more effective in the years ahead than we are today. The fifteen strategic objectives outlined in this strategy can be differentiated as mission objectives and enterprise objectives.

Mission objectives relate to our efforts to predict, penetrate, and preempt threats to our national security and to assist all who make and implement US national security policy, fight our wars, protect our nation, and enforce our laws in the implementation of national policy goals.

Enterprise objectives relate to our capacity to maintain competitive advantages over states and forces that threaten the security of our nation.

Transformation of the Intelligence Community will be driven by the doctrinal principle of integration. Our transformation will be centered on a high-performing intelligence workforce that is:

- Results-focused
- Collaborative
- Bold
- Future-oriented
- Self-evaluating
- Innovative

These six characteristics are interdependent and mutually reinforcing. They will shape our internal policies, programs, institutions, and technologies.

Strategic Objectives

Mission Objectives: To provide accurate and timely intelligence and conduct intelligence programs and activities directed by the President, we must support the following objectives drawn from the *National Security Strategy*:

1. Defeat terrorists at home and abroad by disarming their operational capabilities and seizing the initiative from them by promoting the growth of freedom and democracy.

2. Prevent and counter the spread of weapons of mass destruction.

3. Bolster the growth of democracy and sustain peaceful democratic states.

4. Develop innovative ways to penetrate and analyze the most difficult targets.

5. Anticipate developments of strategic concern and identify opportunities as well as vulnerabilities for decision-makers.

Enterprise Objectives: To transform our capabilities faster than threats emerge, protect what needs to be protected, and perform our duties according to the law, we must:

1. Build an integrated intelligence capability to address threats to the homeland, consistent with US laws and the protection of privacy and civil liberties.

2. Strengthen analytic expertise, methods, and practices; tap expertise wherever it resides; and explore alternative analytic views.

3. Rebalance, integrate, and optimize collection capabilities to meet current and future customer and analytic priorities.

4. Attract, engage, and unify an innovative and results-focused Intelligence Community workforce.

5. Ensure that Intelligence Community members and customers can access the intelligence they need when they need it.

6. Establish new and strengthen existing foreign intelligence relationships to help us meet global security challenges.

7. Create clear, uniform security practices and rules that allow us to work together, protect our nation's secrets, and enable aggressive counterintelligence activities.

8. Exploit path-breaking scientific and research advances that will enable us to maintain and extend intelligence advantages against emerging threats.

9. Learn from our successes and mistakes to anticipate and be ready for new challenges.

10. Eliminate redundancy and programs that add little or no value and re-direct savings to existing and emerging national security priorities.

Strategy Guidance

Mission Objectives

1. Defeat terrorists at home and abroad by disarming their operational capabilities and seizing the initiative from them by promoting the growth of freedom and democracy.

The United States is fighting a war against terror in which our first priority is to identify, disrupt, and destroy terrorist organizations of global reach and attack their leadership, their command, control, and communications, and their material support and finances. Intelligence Community efforts therefore must:

- Integrate and invigorate all US intelligence efforts to identify and disrupt terrorist organizations abroad and within US borders.

- Uncover terrorist plans and intentions, especially those that may involve obtaining or using weapons of mass destruction.

- Deny terrorists operational haven, sanctuary, and political legitimacy by supporting democratization and the rule of law in vulnerable areas.

- Enable those outside the Intelligence Community with valuable counterterrorism information (such as police, corrections officers, and border patrol officers) to contribute to the national counterterrorism effort.

- Create an information sharing environment in which access to terrorism information is matched to the roles, responsibilities, and missions of all organizations engaged in countering terrorism, and is timely, accessible, and relevant to their needs.

The Director of the National Counterterrorism Center will develop a comprehensive national intelligence plan for supporting the nation's war on terror. The plan will identify the roles and responsibilities of each member of the Intelligence Community involved in supporting our national counterterrorism efforts, including their relationships with law enforcement and homeland security authorities. The Program Manager, Information Sharing Environment, will ensure the information needs of federal, state, local, and tribal governments and the private sector are identified and satisfied.

2. Prevent and counter the spread of weapons of mass destruction.

The comprehensive strategy of the US government to combat weapons of mass destruction includes proactive counterproliferation efforts, strengthened nonproliferation efforts to prevent rogue states and terrorists from acquiring these technologies, and effective consequence management to respond to the effects of their use—whether by terrorists or hostile states.

As the WMD Commission stated in its March 2005 report, "There is no single strategy the Intelligence Community can pursue to counter the 'proliferation' menace." Rather, each destructive capability —biological, nuclear, chemical, radiological, or otherwise — will require unique and focused approaches to combating their use. To this end, Intelligence Community efforts must:

- Focus aggressive and innovative collection techniques to close knowledge gaps related to these technologies and associated weapons programs, particularly in the area of bioterrorism, to identify the methods of conveyance, and to prevent them from reaching our shores.

- Reach outside the Intelligence Community for information and expertise relevant to these technologies.

- Integrate the analytic effort within the Intelligence Community, under the leadership of the National Counter-Proliferation Center, by drawing upon the unique expertise and comparative advantages of each Intelligence Community organization.

- Work closely with foreign intelligence services to form a common assessment of threats and develop effective options in response.

- Ensure that weapons of mass destruction intelligence information is coupled with protective countermeasures information and disseminated to all who fight our wars, protect our nation, and enforce our laws.

The Director of the National Counter-Proliferation Center will develop a comprehensive national intelligence plan for supporting the nation's efforts to prevent and counter the development and proliferation of weapons of mass destruction. The plan will identify the roles and responsibilities of each member of the Intelligence Community, including their relationships with law enforcement and homeland security authorities.

Each destructive capability - biological, nuclear, chemical, radiological, or otherwise - will require unique and focused approaches to combating their use.

3. Bolster the growth of democracy and sustain peaceful democratic states.

We have learned to our peril that the lack of freedom in one state endangers the peace and freedom of others and that failed states are a refuge and breeding ground of extremism. Self-sustaining democratic states are essential to world peace and development.

The Intelligence Community — its collectors, analysts, and operators — therefore must:

- Support diplomatic and military efforts (including pre- and post-conflict) when intervention is necessary.

- Forge relationships with new and incipient democracies that can help them strengthen the rule of law and ward off threats to representative government.

- Provide policymakers with an enhanced analytic framework for identifying both the threats to and opportunities for promoting democracy (including free markets and economic development), as well as warning of state failure.

The Deputy Director of National Intelligence for Customer Outcomes will develop a plan to accomplish these objectives. The Deputy Director of National Intelligence for Analysis will contribute to that plan by surveying the analytic expertise and production on democratization and state failure, and the level of Community support now provided to policymakers, identifying knowledge gaps and ways to address them, and improving support to those responsible for monitoring and assisting political and economic development and reducing the danger of state failure. The Deputy Director of National Intelligence for Collection will draft a collection plan, including the use of open sources, responsive to the information needs of this integrated plan.

4. Develop innovative ways to penetrate and analyze the most difficult targets.

America's toughest adversaries know a great deal about our intelligence system and are becoming better at hiding their intentions and capabilities. Some are ruled by closed leadership cadres, and protected by disciplined security and intelligence services. Others are amorphous groups or networks that may share common goals, training, and methods, but which operate independently. The Intelligence Community needs capabilities to penetrate the thinking of both sets of leaders by:

- Making the best use of all-source intelligence, including from open sources, on the most difficult targets.

- Developing new methodologies, including specialized training and career development, for analyzing the capabilities and intentions of hard targets.

- Improving human intelligence and corresponding technical intelligence capabilities.

- Assessing the intelligence capabilities and actions of our adversaries to ensure that an insightful counterintelligence analytic capability helps to penetrate hard targets and understand their leadership cadres.

The Deputy Director of National Intelligence for Collection will develop a plan for improving penetration of hard targets. The Deputy Director of National Intelligence for Analysis will develop a plan to assess the current state of knowledge, identify and close gaps, bolster expertise and research on these targets, and develop new methodologies against them. The National Counterterrorism Center and the National Counterintelligence Executive will devise plans to enhance analysis of terror networks and foreign intelligence establishments and activities. The latter plan will include a means to integrate counterintelligence with other sources to capitalize on opportunities for strategic offensive activities.

5. Anticipate developments of strategic concern and identify opportunities as well as vulnerabilities for decision-makers.

In a world in which developments anywhere can quickly affect American citizens and interests at home and abroad, the Intelligence Community must alert policymakers to problems before they escalate, and provide insights into their causes and effects. Analysis must do more than just describe what is happening and why; it must identify a range of opportunities for (and likely consequences of) diplomatic, military, law enforcement, or homeland security action.

To support policymakers, the Intelligence Community should develop, sustain, and have access to expertise on every region, every transnational security issue, and every threat to the American people. The Intelligence Community will:

- Identify and analyze possible opportunities as well as warn of potential problems.

- Promote deeper cultural understanding, better language proficiency, and scientific and technological knowledge among personnel at all levels.

- Identify gaps in coverage and work to close them through recruitment, training, and consultation with outside expertise.

- Make attention to long-term and strategic analysis a part of every analyst's assigned responsibilities, train analysts to anticipate developments likely to affect US interests, and ensure they are alert to possibilities for timely action.

The Intelligence Community should develop, sustain, and have access to expertise on every region, every transnational security issue, and every threat to the American people.

The Deputy Director of National Intelligence for Analysis will establish a strategic research and analysis unit in the National Intelligence Council; develop procedures to inventory Intelligence Community analytic capabilities on all regions, specified threats, and transnational issues; develop a plan to improve the language skills, scientific and technological skills, and cultural insight of analysts; and work with the analytic components of all Intelligence Community agencies to close gaps, facilitate collaboration, and achieve appropriate balances between long-term and current analysis.

Enterprise Objectives

1. Build an integrated intelligence capability to address threats to the homeland, consistent with US laws and the protection of privacy and civil liberties.

Ubiquitous communications technology, easy international travel, and extremists with the resources and the intent to harm Americans wherever they may reside force us to re-think the way we conduct intelligence collection at home and its relationship with traditional intelligence gathering methods abroad. Consistent with applicable laws and the protection of civil liberties and privacy, US intelligence elements must focus their capabilities to ensure that:

- Intelligence elements in the Departments of Justice and Homeland Security are properly resourced and closely integrated within the larger Intelligence Community.

- All Intelligence Community components assist in facilitating the integration of collection and analysis against terrorists, weapons of mass destruction, and other threats to the homeland.

- State, local, and tribal entities and the private sector are connected to our homeland security and intelligence efforts.

The Deputy Director of National Intelligence for Management will develop a financial, information, and human resource plan for our intelligence capabilities to deal with threats at home that ensures the full and lawful integration of the Intelligence Community elements of the Departments of Justice and Homeland Security with the other Community elements. The Program Manager, Information Sharing Environment, in conjunction with the Chief Information Officer, will develop a plan to facilitate the means for sharing terrorism information among all appropriate federal, state, local, and tribal entities, and the private sector. The Civil Liberties Protection Officer will develop a plan to ensure that improvements to these capabilities are achieved with due regard for the privacy and civil liberties of Americans.

2. Strengthen analytic expertise, methods, and practices; tap expertise wherever it resides; and explore alternative analytic views.

To avoid intelligence failures, the analytic judgments presented to policymakers must be the product of an enterprise that values differing perspectives, nurtures and rewards expertise, and is agile and innovative in the way it deploys and utilizes that expertise.

To strengthen and sustain Intelligence Community analytic capabilities and to ensure that appropriate expertise is brought to bear efficiently and constructively, the Intelligence Community must:

- Build and sustain the expertise and capacity of the Intelligence Community's analyst "corps," leveraging the unique capabilities of each component, and fostering cross-agency collaboration at all levels.

- Utilize expertise from outside the Intelligence Community to inform judgments and to bolster areas where knowledge is lacking in the Community.

- Improve analytic methods and practices across the Community, ensuring rigor and the exploration of alternative analysis.

The Deputy Director of National Intelligence for Analysis will develop a plan to identify expertise inside and outside government, establish virtual teams of experts and interested analysts from across the Intelligence Community and US government, improve cooperation between analysis and collection, improve analytic methods and practices, and ensure analytic integrity. The plan will also address new processes to allow the Office of the Director of National Intelligence to manage key intelligence issues, including inventorying analytic leads and activities for high priority issues, identifying knowledge gaps, and working with collection managers to close them.

3. Rebalance, integrate, and optimize collection capabilities to meet current and future customer and analytic priorities.

Our technical means of collecting information must remain unmatched. They allow us to avert conflict, expand peace, and win wars. The nation gains when our technical systems are developed for multiple purposes, but long development schedules and changing requirements undermine our agility and resources. Accordingly, the Intelligence Community must:

- Expand collection and analysis from open sources, and manage them as integrated intelligence activities.

- Establish a national clandestine service to integrate all the elements of human source collection in accord with the highest traditions of professionalism and intellectual prowess.

- Rebalance the technical collection architecture to improve responsiveness to user requirements; enhance flexibility and survivability; and provide new sources and methods for current and emerging targets.

- Expand the reporting of information of intelligence value from state, local, and tribal law enforcement entities and private sector stakeholders.

The Deputy Director of National Intelligence for Collection will develop a comprehensive plan for achieving a new balance among our various collection methods—open, human, and technical sources—while taking account of the differing legal and policy framework for collection within the United States. The plan will reflect the changed nature of the threats we face, the vast opportunities of the information age, and new non-traditional sources of information now available. The Foreign Denial and Deception Committee will complete a plan for countering denial and deception practices deployed against us.

4. Attract, engage, and unify an innovative and results-focused Intelligence Community workforce.

The complexity of the challenges the United States faces in the 21st century will require those who serve in the Intelligence Community, both military and civilian, to apply expertise against a wide range of threats, and to become more adept and innovative in acquiring, analyzing, and communicating the knowledge that policymakers need.

In order to ensure the Intelligence Community is able to meet these expectations, it must:

- Recruit exceptional individuals from a diverse talent pool, train and develop them to meet the challenges they will face, and then deploy them in ways that maximize their talents and potential.

- Reward expertise, excellence, and commitment to service; provide opportunities for professional growth and leadership development, and encourage initiative, innovation, resourcefulness, and resilience among the civilian and military members of the Intelligence Community and those who lead them.

- Build an Intelligence Community-wide culture that values the abilities of each of its members and provides them developmental opportunities across the Intelligence Community in accord with their aptitudes and aspirations.

The Chief Human Capital Officer, in partnership with the Chief Training and Education Officer, will develop an Intelligence Community Strategic Human Capital Plan that will enable Community elements to: identify mission-critical human resource requirements; train, develop, and promote Community professionals according to rigorous, competency-based standards; select a senior leadership cadre that promotes high performance, employee engagement, information sharing, and collaboration; and develop evaluation and reward systems that reinforce excellence among professionals and those who lead them.

5. Ensure that Intelligence Community members and customers can access the intelligence they need when they need it.

The Intelligence Reform and Terrorism Prevention Act of 2004 directed the Director of National Intelligence to "ensure maximum availability of and access to intelligence information." We must ensure maximum interoperability inside the Community while creating effective, flexible links to customers. Intelligence Community efforts must:

- Remove impediments to information sharing within the Community, and establish policies that reflect need-to-share (versus need-to-know) for all data, removing the "ownership" by agency of intelligence information.

- Build a user-friendly system that allows customers to find needed intelligence and access it immediately.

- Develop flexible and secure networks adaptable to a rapidly changing environment and capable of getting intelligence in an unclassified form to non-traditional customers such as state, local, and tribal governments and the private sector.

- Create an intelligence "cyber community" where analysts, collectors, and customers can interact swiftly and easily in considering classified information.

The Deputy Director of National Intelligence for Customer Outcomes will oversee the development of plans to provide maximum access to intelligence information among Intelligence Community customers, consistent with applicable laws and the protection of civil liberties and privacy. The Program Manager, Information Sharing Environment, will create a plan to ensure that the Information Sharing Environment provides the functional equivalent of, or otherwise supports, a decentralized, distributed, and coordinated environment as described in Section 1016(b)(2) of the Intelligence Reform and Terrorism Prevention Act of 2004. The Chief Information Officer will develop a plan to ensure that activities and procurements relating to the information technology infrastructure and enterprise architecture of the Intelligence Community meet the need to share information more broadly.

6. Establish new and strengthen existing foreign intelligence relationships to help us meet global security challenges.

Since our most serious national security challenges are transnational, the Community must enlist like-minded nations to extend our reach. As the *National Security Strategy* states, "no nation can build a safer, better world alone." To this end, we must:

- Engage and invigorate friendly foreign intelligence services' efforts that could aid in the identification and disruption of terrorist organizations abroad and within US borders.

- Coordinate closely with foreign intelligence services to inform a common assessment of threats and options in response.

- Ensure that insights gained from our foreign intelligence relationships inform intelligence judgments and develop effective options in response.

The Deputy Director of National Intelligence for Customer Outcomes will direct the development of a strategic plan on foreign intelligence relationships to ensure that the relationships are being adequately coordinated and employed to meet national security threats. This plan will include a process to identify existing gaps as well as to determine if new foreign intelligence relationships need to be established or existing relationships strengthened.

7. Create clear, uniform security practices and rules that allow us to work together, protect our nation's secrets, and enable aggressive counterintelligence activities.

The Intelligence Community must dramatically change the basis of its security and counterintelligence policies in order to remain effective. We must rigorously assess threat, vulnerability, and protection requirements to further overall Community objectives. Intelligence Community efforts must:

- Redefine classification guidelines to allow for a large body of "sensitive" information with flexible use and sharing arrangements, and a smaller body of "restricted" information available to fewer personnel.

- Establish uniform and reciprocal Intelligence Community guidance on security issues of common concern, including access to facilities, and electronic access to systems and databases.

- Institute new procedures, including innovative security assessment and reliability monitoring, permitting agencies to expeditiously assess personnel with potential vulnerabilities.

- Ensure the various Intelligence Community elements conducting counterintelligence activities act as a cohesive whole to undertake aggressive, unified counterintelligence operations.

The Intelligence Community must dramatically change the basis of its security and counterintelligence policies in order to remain effective.

The Deputy Director of National Intelligence for Management will develop a plan for changing physical, information, and personnel security policies impeding the Intelligence Community's ability to achieve its mission and enterprise objectives. The National Counterintelligence Executive, in the plan for implementing the National Counterintelligence Strategy, will describe how the Community will undertake aggressive counterintelligence operations with greater unity of effort. The Chief Information Officer will develop a plan for new security policies that promote information sharing across the Intelligence Community.

8. Exploit path-breaking scientific and research advances that will enable us to maintain and extend intelligence advantages against emerging threats.

Globalization and accelerating scientific and technological progress threaten to erode the Intelligence Community's technical collection means, to undermine our ability to identify/access world-class scientific expertise, and to degrade our ability to exploit emerging technological advances.

The Intelligence Community's ability to identify and leverage cutting-edge scientific and technological research depends on our capacity to forecast technological trends, interact with leading researchers, and gain early access to innovative concepts and designs. To this end, Intelligence Community efforts must:

- Establish a centrally led, but de-centrally executed, process for Intelligence Community scientific and technological activities.

- Deepen technical expertise and strengthen advanced research and development programs within the agencies.

- Identify high risk, high reward research for special emphasis by the Office of the Director of National Intelligence, particularly in the "white spaces" between various agency efforts.

- Foster joint development among agency research efforts, where appropriate.

The Associate Director of National Intelligence for Science and Technology will develop a plan for leading the Intelligence Community's science and technology resources and activities. The plan will identify the roles and responsibilities for each member of the Intelligence Community engaged in scientific and technological activities.

Globalization and accelerating scientific and technological progress threaten to erode the Intelligence Community's technical collection means...

9. Learn from our successes and mistakes to anticipate and be ready for new challenges.

The Intelligence Community must continuously improve its ability to record, assess, and learn from its performance, in part by establishing metrics to measure its performance. The process of conducting performance reviews and learning from both successes and failures should help identify systemic shortcomings. In addition to assimilating lessons, the Community must also assess its readiness. Intelligence Community efforts must:

- Create a lessons-learned function to assess the effectiveness of the Community's activities as a "system of systems" in supporting national policy goals.

- Establish a rigorous evaluation process that determines how well individual strategic plans meet their stated goals and how effectively they support the relevant mission and enterprise objectives.

- Incorporate into each agency's strategic plan a readiness component addressing crises and contingencies.

- Create a robust command and control system for the Director of National Intelligence.

The Deputy Director of National Intelligence for Management will develop plans to assess the Community's performance against mission and enterprise objectives, establish a Community-wide lessons-learned function, and guide the improvement of readiness within the agencies. The Chief Information Officer will develop a plan to ensure the functioning of the Director of National Intelligence's command and control system in all contingencies.

10. Eliminate redundancy and programs that add little or no value and re-direct savings to existing and emerging national security priorities.

The Intelligence Community is a vast enterprise, with areas of overlapping missions and expertise. In some instances, the overlap adds value; in others it consumes resources more appropriately directed to the Intelligence Community member having the mission at its core, or to emerging national security threats.

The Intelligence Community must manage its resources by examining national security priorities, both short and long term, and quickly adapt to changes in

18

them. The Community must also revise its financial procedures and processes; existing budget reports are not providing the level of consistency required for appropriate oversight. To this end, the Intelligence Community must:

- Standardize, synchronize, and coordinate financial reporting in order to provide a comprehensive and auditable record of Community expenditures.

- Assess the current program development process with emphasis on evaluating how program submissions are aligned against objectives.

- Eliminate mission and program redundancy that adds little or no value.

- End programs/projects that no longer meet national security priorities or that do not deliver as promised.

- Consolidate similar programs and missions under one Community lead.

- Redirect resources saved through consolidation and terminated programs to existing and emerging threats.

- Ensure that new systems are developed in compliance with an Intelligence Community Enterprise Architecture.

The Deputy Director of National Intelligence for Management will develop a plan to identify and eliminate unnecessary redundancy and low value programs within the Intelligence Community. The plan will also address how to identify missions and programs where resources should be redirected to meet new and emerging national security threats and to enhance secure intelligence capabilities for organizations that function primarily in the United States. The plan will specify the roles and responsibilities of Intelligence Community members engaged in resource management and program development to continually examine their programs and missions and to collaborate with one another in arriving at recommendations for mission adjustments, program consolidations or terminations, and areas ripe for redirection of resources. It will also describe how to strengthen the Community's financial management systems with the goal of achieving comprehensive audits of the major intelligence programs.

Next Steps

These strategic objectives will guide Intelligence Community policy, planning, collection, analysis, operations, programming, acquisition, budgeting, and execution. They will be overseen by senior officials of the Office of the Director of National Intelligence, but will be implemented through an integrated Intelligence Community effort to capitalize on the comparative advantages of constituent organizations.

- The Deputy Director of National Intelligence for Management will develop a strategic planning and evaluation process for the Intelligence Community.

- The Fiscal Year 2008 planning, programming, and performance guidance will reflect these mission and enterprise objectives. Ongoing program and budget activities for Fiscal Years 2006 and 2007 will adjust to these objectives to the maximum extent possible.

These strategic objectives will guide Intelligence Community policy, planning, collection, analysis, operations, programming, acquisition, budgeting, and execution.

FOR INFORMATION CONTACT:
OFFICE OF THE DIRECTOR OF NATIONAL INTELLIGENCE
WASHINGTON, DC 20511

WWW.ODNI.GOV